MAYA ANGELOU

A Little Golden Book® Biography

By Anne Wynter

Illustrated by Courtney Lovett

A GOLDEN BOOK • NEW YORK

Text copyright © 2025 by Anne Wynter
Cover art and interior illustrations copyright © 2025 by Courtney Lovett
All rights reserved. Published in the United States by Golden Books, an imprint of
Random House Children's Books, a division of Penguin Random House LLC, 1745 Broadway,
New York, NY 10019. Golden Books, A Golden Book, A Little Golden Book, the G colophon,
and the distinctive gold spine are registered trademarks of Penguin Random House LLC.
rhcbooks.com
Educators and librarians, for a variety of teaching tools, visit us at RHTeachersLibrarians.com
Library of Congress Control Number: 2023930107
ISBN 978-0-593-64837-7 (trade) — ISBN 978-0-593-64838-4 (ebook)
Printed in the United States of America
10 9 8 7 6 5 4 3 2 1

Marguerite Annie Johnson was born on April 4, 1928, in St. Louis, Missouri. Her older brother, Bailey, called her "Mya sister," which eventually turned into the name Maya.

When Maya was three years old and Bailey was four, their parents sent them to live with their grandmother— who they called Momma—in the small town of Stamps, Arkansas.

The siblings took the long train ride from St. Louis
to Stamps all by themselves. Kind passengers gave the
children chicken and potato salad to eat during the trip.
Pullman porters—Black men who worked onboard the
trains—made sure Maya and Bailey changed trains at
the right stations.

In Stamps, Maya and Bailey lived with Momma and their uncle Willie in the general store Momma owned. Momma taught Maya how to read, and Uncle Willie quizzed the siblings on multiplication tables. Maya was so good at figuring out math problems that Momma called her "my little professor."

When she was eight years old, Maya stopped speaking.
Even though she kept her words to herself, she fell in love
with the words of great writers, especially plays and poems
by William Shakespeare. She read every single book in
the Black school library and all the books she could get
from the white school library.

A teacher named Bertha Flowers began inviting Maya over to her house. She served lemonade and cookies and read books and poems to Maya. She encouraged Maya to try reading out loud. Mrs. Flowers explained that the human voice can give words a deeper meaning.

Maya began to speak again.

When Maya was thirteen, she and Bailey moved to San Francisco, California, to live with their mother. Maya received a scholarship to study theater and dance, but she left school for a while to get a job.

She wanted to be a streetcar conductor. Maya pictured
herself riding along San Francisco's hilly streets, collecting
money from passengers, and wearing a fancy uniform.

She was told that Black people couldn't work on the
streetcars, but Maya wouldn't give up. After asking for
a job again and again, she was finally hired as one of the
first Black female conductors on San Francisco's streetcars—
and she was only sixteen years old!

During her senior year of high school, Maya's son, Clyde Bailey Johnson, was born. She called him Guy. To support the two of them, she held several different jobs. She was a waitress, a cook, a singer, and a dancer.

One day, she auditioned for the opera *Porgy and Bess*—
and got the part! Maya joined the cast and traveled
around the world, performing in Canada, Italy, Spain,
Egypt, and several other countries.

Maya also wrote. She wrote poems, music, short stories, and song lyrics. Her friends suggested that she move to New York City and join the Harlem Writers Guild. She took their advice and became an even bettter writer.

She was inspired when she heard Dr. Martin Luther King Jr. speak about changing the world through nonviolence. Soon, Maya began using her writing and her voice to fight for equal rights for Black people.

Maya's friends loved hearing her tell stories about her childhood. One day, an editor asked her to write a book. At first, Maya didn't think it was a good idea, but finally, she agreed. She called her autobiography *I Know Why the Caged Bird Sings* and wrote about her experiences from the ages of three through sixteen. People everywhere read it and loved it. Maya's book became a classic.

Maya kept writing. She wrote movies, plays, and more than thirty books, including poetry collections, children's books, cookbooks, and six more autobiographies.

Maya kept performing. She appeared on Broadway, in movies, and in television shows, including the miniseries *Roots*. She also became a college professor and speaker, sharing her words and knowledge with students and audiences. Maya once said, "When you learn, teach. When you get, give."

On the cold morning of January 20, 1993, Maya read her poem "On the Pulse of Morning" at the inauguration of President Bill Clinton. The poem, which Maya wrote specifically for the occasion, spoke of the country's difficult past and bright future. Sharing her poem in a clear, powerful voice, Maya made people feel hopeful and inspired.

Maya won many awards for writing and performing. She didn't go to college, but she received more than fifty honorary degrees from colleges and universities around the country. And President Barack Obama presented her with the 2010 Presidential Medal of Freedom.

Maya Angelou died on May 28, 2014. She is so respected and beloved that she continues to be honored today.

In 2022, Maya became the first Black woman to have her image featured on a US quarter.

When she met her fans, Maya would often sign
her books with her name and a single word: joy!

She found joy in many parts of her extraordinary
life, and her writing continues to bring joy to people
around the world.